Taylor

PRESENTED TO

Love, Mike & Pam

FROM

5 - 2 - 2017

DATE

40 Days
with
Jesus

by

Sarah Young

truly a light &
beneficial for you!

THOMAS NELSON
Since 1798

NASHVILLE   MEXICO CITY   RIO DE JANEIRO

Published in Nashville, Tennessee by Thomas Nelson. Thomas Nelson is a trademark of HarperCollins Christian Publishing.

Excerpts taken from *Jesus Calling* and *Jesus Lives* by Sarah Young. Used by permission.

Thomas Nelson titles may be purchased in bulk for educational, business, fund-raising, or sales promotional use. For information, please e-mail SpecialMarkets@ThomasNelson.com.

Unless otherwise noted, Scripture quotations used in this book are from: The *Holy Bible, New International Version*®. © 1973, 1978, 1984, by Biblica, Inc.™ Used by permission of Zondervan. All rights reserved worldwide.

Other Scripture references are from the following sources:
King James Version (KJV); NEW KING JAMES VERSION (NKJV), © 1982, Thomas Nelson; New American Standard Bible (NASB), © 1960, 1962, 1963, 1968, 1971, 1972, 1973, 1975, 1977, 1995 by The Lockman Foundation; The Amplified® Bible (AMP), © 1954, 1958, 1962, 1964, 1965, 1987 by The Lockman Foundation. Used by permission.

Cover design by Brand Navigation LLC; www.brandnavigation.com

ISBN-13: 978-1-4041-8994-2 (with display)
ISBN-13: 978-0-529-10493-9

Printed in the United States of America
16 17 18 POL 7

Introduction

———⊸✦⊷———

Written as if Jesus is speaking to you personally, *40 Days with Jesus* is designed to help you deepen your relationship with God. Each day of this journey will offer you a reminder that He is always with you. These excerpts from the bestselling devotionals, *Jesus Calling* and *Jesus Lives* by Sarah Young, bring to light that we can live each day aware of Jesus' Presence.

May the 40 days you spend reading this booklet draw you closer to the Savior and strengthen your relationship with Him. May your time be blessed and your spirit renewed; may you be transformed, challenged, and restored. And may your life be immeasurably enriched by the One who gave it all—for you. Do you hear Him calling?

TASTE AND SEE THAT I AM GOOD. The more intimately you experience Me, the more convinced you become of My goodness. *I am the Living One who sees you* and longs to participate in your life. I am training you to find Me in each moment and to be a channel of My loving Presence. Sometimes My blessings come to you in mysterious ways: through pain and trouble. At such times you can know My goodness only through your trust in Me. Understanding will fail you, but trust will keep you close to Me.

Thank Me for the gift of My Peace, a gift of such immense proportions that you cannot fathom its depth or breadth. When I appeared to My disciples after the resurrection, it was Peace that I communicated first of all. I knew this was their deepest need: to calm their fears and clear their minds. I also speak Peace to you, for I know your anxious thoughts. Listen to Me! Tune out other voices, so that you can hear Me more clearly. I designed you to dwell in Peace all day, every day. Draw near to Me; receive My Peace.

Taste and see that the LORD is good;
    blessed is the man who takes refuge in him.

PSALM 34:8

Let the peace of Christ rule in your hearts, since as members of one body you were called to peace. And be thankful.

COLOSSIANS 3:15

FOR REFLECTION: GENESIS 16:13–14 (AMP); JOHN 20:19

LET MY LOVE ENFOLD YOU in the radiance of My Glory. Sit still in the Light of My Presence, and receive My Peace. These quiet moments with Me transcend time, accomplishing far more than you can imagine. Bring Me the sacrifice of your time, and watch to see how abundantly I bless you and your loved ones.

Through the intimacy of our relationship, you are being *transformed* from the inside out. As you keep your focus on Me, I form you into the one I desire you to be. Your part is to yield to My creative work in you, neither resisting it nor trying to speed it up. Enjoy the tempo of a God-breathed life by letting Me set the pace. Hold My hand in childlike trust, and the way before you will open up step by step.

And we, who with unveiled faces all reflect the Lord's glory, are being transformed into his likeness with ever-increasing glory, which comes from the Lord, who is the Spirit.

2 CORINTHIANS 3:18

Yet I am always with you;
    you hold me by my right hand.
You guide me with your counsel,
    and afterward you will take me into glory.

PSALM 73:23–24

FOR REFLECTION: HEBREWS 13:15

FOLLOW ME ONE STEP AT A TIME. That is all I require of you. In fact, that is the only way to move through this space/time world. You see huge mountains looming, and you start wondering how you're going to scale those heights. Meanwhile, because you're not looking where you're going, you stumble on the easy path where I am leading you now. As I help you get back on your feet, you tell Me how worried you are about the cliffs up ahead. But you don't know what will happen today, much less tomorrow. Our path may take an abrupt turn, leading you away from those mountains. There may be an easier way up the mountains than is visible from this distance. If I do lead you up the cliffs, I will equip you thoroughly for that strenuous climb. *I will even give My angels charge over you, to preserve you in all your ways.*

Keep your mind on the present journey, enjoying My Presence. *Walk by faith, not by sight,* trusting Me to open up the way before you.

For He will give His angels [especial] charge over you to accompany and defend and preserve you in all your ways [of obedience and service]. They shall bear you up on their hands, lest you dash your foot against a stone.

PSALM 91:11–12 (AMP)

For we walk by faith, not by sight.

2 CORINTHIANS 5:7 (NKJV)

FOR REFLECTION: PSALM 18:29

YOU ARE MY BELOVED CHILD. *I chose you before the foundation of the world*, to walk with Me along paths designed uniquely for you. Concentrate on keeping in step with Me, instead of trying to anticipate My plans for you. If you trust that My plans are *to prosper you and not to harm you*, you can relax and enjoy the present moment.

Your hope and your future are rooted in heaven, where eternal ecstasy awaits you. Nothing can rob you of your inheritance of unimaginable riches and well-being. Sometimes I grant you glimpses of your glorious future, to encourage you and spur you on. But your main focus should be staying close to Me. I set the pace in keeping with your needs and My purposes.

Just as He chose us in Him before the foundation of the world, that we should be holy and without blame before Him in love.

EPHESIANS 1:4 (NKJV)

"For I know the plans I have for you," declares the LORD, "plans to prosper you and not to harm you, plans to give you hope and a future."

JEREMIAH 29:11

And you also were included in Christ when you heard the word of truth, the gospel of your salvation. Having believed, you were marked in him with a seal, the promised Holy Spirit, who is a deposit guaranteeing our inheritance until the redemption of those who are God's possession—to the praise of his glory.

EPHESIANS 1:13–14

FOR REFLECTION: PROVERBS 16:9

I AM THE RESURRECTION AND THE LIFE; all lasting Life emanates from Me. People search for life in many wrong ways: chasing after fleeting pleasures, accumulating possessions and wealth, trying to deny the inevitable effects of aging. Meanwhile, I freely offer abundant Life to everyone who turns toward Me. As you *come to Me and take My yoke upon you*, I fill you with My very Life. This is how I choose to live in the world and accomplish My purposes. This is also how I bless you with *Joy unspeakable and full of Glory.* The Joy is Mine, and the Glory is Mine; but I bestow them on you as you live in My Presence, inviting Me to live fully in you.

———◆———

Jesus said to her, "I am the resurrection and the life. He who believes in me will live, even though he dies."

JOHN 11:25

"Come to me, all you who are weary and burdened, and I will give you rest. Take my yoke upon you and learn from me, for I am gentle and humble in heart, and you will find rest for your souls."

MATTHEW 11:28–29

Whom having not seen, ye love; in whom, though now ye see him not, yet believing, ye rejoice with joy unspeakable and full of glory: receiving the end of your faith, even the salvation of your souls.

1 PETER 1:8–9 (KJV)

MY KINGDOM CANNOT BE SHAKEN! This present world seems to be shaking more and more, leaving you off-balance much of the time. As you worship Me, however, your perspective changes and you regain your balance. To worship Me *acceptably with reverence and awe*, thankfulness is essential. I designed you to *be thankful* on a daily, moment-by-moment basis. You need to resist the temptation to grumble when things don't go as you would like. Remember that I, your God, am *a consuming fire*. If you saw Me in all My Glory, you would be much too awestruck to venture even the tiniest complaint.

My unshakable kingdom is for all people who love Me, who know Me as Savior. This everlasting kingdom consists of things that *no eye has seen, no ear has heard, no mind has conceived*. I have prepared infinite, wondrous delights *for those who love Me*. Moreover, at the end of the age *I will come back and take you to be with Me so that you may be where I am*. Let these precious promises ignite your thankfulness, till you are aglow with My living Presence—shining brightly in this dark world.

Therefore, since we are receiving a kingdom that cannot be shaken, let us be thankful, and so worship God acceptably with reverence and awe, for our God is a consuming fire.

HEBREWS 12:28–29

FOR REFLECTION: EXODUS 24:17 (NKJV);
1 CORINTHIANS 2:9; JOHN 14:3

I AM IMMANUEL—GOD WITH YOU—*an ever-present Help in trouble.* No matter what may happen, I am sufficient to provide whatever you need. Instead of imagining how you might respond to terrible things that could happen, draw your mind back to the present and take refuge in My Presence. I am much like a mother hen, eager to cover you with My protective pinions. As you snuggle *under My wings*, you will not only *find refuge*; you will also discover a growing ability to trust Me. It is in closeness to Me that you realize how trustworthy I am.

Remember that I am both your Rock and your Redeemer. Though I am impregnable in My vast strength, I became a vulnerable Man so I could redeem you from your sins. The more you take refuge in Me, the more aware you become of My overflowing Love. In Me you are utterly safe, for I am your Rock of everlasting Love!

May the words of my mouth and the meditation of my heart be pleasing in your sight, O LORD, my Rock and my Redeemer.

PSALM 19:14

FOR REFLECTION: PSALM 46:1–2;
MATTHEW 23:37 (NKJV); PSALM 91:4 (AMP)

I WILL NEVER LEAVE YOU OR FORSAKE YOU. Many of My followers think they have to jump through all the right hoops to "stay in fellowship" with Me. If that were true, they would never be able to enjoy My Presence. They would have to be perfect to gain an audience with Me. Instead of striving to be good enough, I invite you to come confidently into My bright Presence.

If you *walk in the Light as I am in the Light, My blood continually cleanses you from all sin.* When you become aware of sins, I want you to confess them and seek My help in making needed changes. Nonetheless, your status with Me is not based on confessing your sins quickly enough or thoroughly enough. The only thing that keeps you right with Me is My perfect righteousness, which I gave you freely and permanently when you joined My royal family.

Walking in the Light of My Presence blesses you in many ways. Good things are better and bad things more bearable when you share them with Me. As you bask in My Love-Light, you are better able to love others and enjoy fellowship with them. You are less likely to stumble or fall, because sins are garishly obvious in My holy Light. As you walk in this Light with Me, I encourage you to *exult in My righteousness.*

———≫◦≪———

Blessed are those who have learned to acclaim you, who walk in the light of your presence, O LORD. They rejoice in your name all day long; they exult in your righteousness.

PSALM 89:15–16

FOR REFLECTION: HEBREWS 13:5; 1 JOHN 1:7 (NKJV)

I AM THE RISEN ONE who shines upon you always. You worship a living Deity, not some idolatrous, man-made image. Your relationship with Me is meant to be vibrant and challenging, as I invade more and more areas of your life. Do not fear change, for I am making you a *new creation, with old things passing away and new things continually on the horizon.* When you cling to old ways and sameness, you resist My work within you. I want you to embrace all that I am doing in your life, finding your security in Me alone.

It is easy to make an idol of routine, finding security within the boundaries you build around your life. Although each day contains twenty-four hours, every single one presents a unique set of circumstances. Don't try to force-fit today into yesterday's mold. Instead, ask Me to open your eyes, so you can find all I have prepared for you in this precious day of Life.

The angel said to the women, "Do not be afraid, for I know that you are looking for Jesus, who was crucified. He is not here; he has risen, just as he said. Come and see the place where he lay. Then go quickly and tell his disciples: 'He has risen from the dead and is going ahead of you into Galilee. There you will see him.' Now I have told you."

MATTHEW 28:5–7

Therefore, if anyone is in Christ, he is a new creation; the old has gone, the new has come!

2 CORINTHIANS 5:17

YOU ARE A CHILD OF GOD, and you are Mine forever. Someday you will *see Me as I am*—face to Face in Glory. You have been a member of My royal family since the moment you trusted Me as Savior. I am training you in the ways of My kingdom: *to be made new in the attitude of your mind; to put on the new self, created to be like Me.* Although your new self is being conformed to My image, this process does not erase the essence of who you are. On the contrary, the more you become *like Me*, the more you develop into the unique person I designed you to be.

Since you are part of My royal family, you're a *fellow-heir with Me—sharing My inheritance.* However, *you must share My suffering if you are to share My Glory.* You don't need to search for ways to suffer. Living in this broken world provides ample opportunity to experience pain of many kinds. When adversity comes your way, search for Me in the midst of your struggles. Ask Me to help you suffer well, in a manner worthy of royalty. Everything you endure can help you become more like Me. Remember the ultimate goal: *You will see My Face in righteousness—and be satisfied!*

―――――◦◦◦◦―――――

Beloved, now we are children of God; and it has not yet been revealed what we shall be, but we know that when He is revealed, we shall be like Him, for we shall see Him as He is.

1 JOHN 3:2 (NKJV)

FOR REFLECTION: EPHESIANS 4:22–24;
ROMANS 8:17 (AMP); PSALM 17:15 (NKJV)

I SPEAK TO YOU FROM THE DEPTHS OF YOUR BEING. Hear Me saying soothing words of Peace, assuring you of My Love. Do not listen to voices of accusation, for they are not from Me. I speak to you in love-tones, lifting you up. My Spirit convicts cleanly, without crushing words of shame. Let the Spirit take charge of your mind, combing out tangles of deception. Be transformed by the truth that I live within you.

The Light of My Presence is shining upon you, in benedictions of Peace. Let My Light shine in you; don't dim it with worries or fears. Holiness is letting Me live through you. Since I dwell in you, you are fully equipped to be holy. Pause before responding to people or situations, giving My Spirit space to act through you. Hasty words and actions leave no room for Me; this is atheistic living. I want to inhabit all your moments—gracing your thoughts, words, and behavior.

———⟫●⟪———

Therefore, there is now no condemnation for those who are in Christ Jesus, because through Christ Jesus the law of the Spirit of life set me free from the law of sin and death.

ROMANS 8:1–2

To them God has chosen to make known among the Gentiles the glorious riches of this mystery, which is Christ in you, the hope of glory.

COLOSSIANS 1:27

FOR REFLECTION: 1 CORINTHIANS 6:19

DAY 12

I AM CALLING YOU to a life of constant communion with Me. Basic training includes learning to live above your circumstances, even while interacting on that cluttered plane of life. You yearn for a simplified lifestyle, so that your communication with Me can be uninterrupted. But I challenge you to relinquish the fantasy of an uncluttered world. Accept each day just as it comes, and find Me in the midst of it all.

Talk with Me about every aspect of your day, including your feelings. Remember that your ultimate goal is not to control or fix everything around you; it is to keep communing with Me. A successful day is one in which you have stayed in touch with Me, even if many things remain undone at the end of the day. Do not let your to-do list (written or mental) become an idol directing your life. Instead, ask My Spirit to guide you moment by moment. He will keep you close to Me.

Pray continually.

1 THESSALONIANS 5:17

In all your ways acknowledge him,
  and he will make your paths straight.

PROVERBS 3:6

HEAVEN IS BOTH PRESENT AND FUTURE. As you walk along your life-path holding My hand, you are already in touch with the essence of heaven: nearness to Me. You can also find many hints of heaven along your pathway, because the earth is radiantly alive with My Presence. Shimmering sunshine awakens your heart, gently reminding you of My brilliant Light. Birds and flowers, trees and skies evoke praises to My holy Name. Keep your eyes and ears fully open as you journey with Me.

At the end of your life-path is an entrance to heaven. Only I know when you will reach that destination, but I am preparing you for it each step of the way. The absolute certainty of your heavenly home gives you Peace and Joy, to help you along your journey. You know that you will reach your home in My perfect timing: not one moment too soon or too late. Let the hope of heaven encourage you, as you walk along the path of Life with Me.

But Christ has indeed been raised from the dead, the firstfruits of those who have fallen asleep. For since death came through a man, the resurrection of the dead comes also through a man. For as in Adam all die, so in Christ all will be made alive. But each in his own turn: Christ, the firstfruits; then, when he comes, those who belong to him.

1 CORINTHIANS 15:20–23

FOR REFLECTION: HEBREWS 6:19

PEACE IS MY CONTINUAL GIFT TO YOU. It flows abundantly from My throne of grace. Just as the Israelites could not store up manna for the future but had to gather it daily, so it is with My Peace. The day-by-day collecting of manna kept My people aware of their dependence on Me. Similarly, I give you sufficient Peace for the present, when you come to me *by prayer and petition with thanksgiving.* If I gave you permanent Peace, independent of My Presence, you might fall into the trap of self-sufficiency. May that never be!

I have designed you to need Me moment by moment. As your awareness of your neediness increases, so does your realization of My abundant sufficiency. *I can meet every one of your needs* without draining My resources at all. *Approach My throne of grace with bold confidence,* receiving My Peace with a thankful heart.

Do not be anxious about anything, but in everything, by prayer and petition, with thanksgiving, present your requests to God. And the peace of God, which transcends all understanding, will guard your hearts and your minds in Christ Jesus. . . . And my God will meet all your needs according to his glorious riches in Christ Jesus.

PHILIPPIANS 4:6–7, 19

Let us then approach the throne of grace with confidence, so that we may receive mercy and find grace to help us in our time of need.

HEBREWS 4:16

FOR REFLECTION: EXODUS 16:14–20

WAITING, TRUSTING, AND HOPING are intricately connected, like golden strands interwoven to form a strong chain. Trusting is the central strand, because it is the response from My children that I desire the most. Waiting and hoping embellish the central strand and strengthen the chain that connects you to Me. Waiting for Me to work, with your eyes on Me, is evidence that you really do trust Me. If you mouth the words "I trust You" while anxiously trying to make things go your way, your words ring hollow. Hoping is future-directed, connecting you to your inheritance in heaven. However, the benefits of hope fall fully on you in the present.

Because you are Mine, you don't just pass time in your waiting. You can wait expectantly, in hopeful trust. Keep your "antennae" out to pick up even the faintest glimmer of My Presence.

"Do not let your hearts be troubled. Trust in God; trust also in me."

JOHN 14:1

Wait for the LORD;
    be strong and take heart
    and wait for the LORD.

PSALM 27:14

FOR REFLECTION: HEBREWS 6:18–20

I AM WITH YOU, watching over you constantly. I am Immanuel (*God with you*); My Presence enfolds you in radiant Love. Nothing, including the brightest blessings and the darkest trials, can separate you from Me. Some of My children find Me more readily during dark times, when difficulties force them to depend on Me. Others feel closer to Me when their lives are filled with good things. They respond with thanksgiving and praise, thus opening wide the door to My Presence.

I know precisely what you need to draw nearer to Me. Go through each day looking for what I have prepared for you. Accept every event as My hand-tailored provision for your needs. When you view your life this way, the most reasonable response is to be thankful. Do not reject any of My gifts; find Me in every situation.

"The virgin will be with child and will give birth to a son, and they will call him Immanuel"—which means, "God with us."

MATTHEW 1:23

So then, just as you received Christ Jesus as Lord, continue to live in him, rooted and built up in him, strengthened in the faith as you were taught, and overflowing with thankfulness.

COLOSSIANS 2:6–7

I HAVE LOVED YOU with an everlasting Love. Before time began, I knew you. For years you swam around in a sea of meaningless-ness, searching for Love, hoping for hope. All that time I was pursuing you, aching to embrace you in My compassionate arms.

When time was right, I revealed Myself to you. I lifted you out of that sea of despair and set you down on a firm foundation. Sometimes you felt naked—exposed to the revealing Light of My Presence. I wrapped an ermine robe around you: *My robe of righteousness.* I sang you a Love song, whose beginning and end are veiled in eternity. I infused meaning into your mind and harmony into your heart. Join Me in singing My song. Together we will draw others *out of darkness into My marvelous Light.*

The LORD appeared to us in the past, saying: "I have loved you with an everlasting love; I have drawn you with loving-kindness."

JEREMIAH 31:3

I delight greatly in the LORD; my soul rejoices in my God. For he has clothed me with garments of salvation and arrayed me in a robe of righteousness, as a bridegroom adorns his head like a priest, and as a bride adorns herself with her jewels.

ISAIAH 61:10

FOR REFLECTION: 1 PETER 2:9 (NKJV)

I AM LIFE AND LIGHT IN ABUNDANCE. As you spend time "soaking" in My Presence, you are energized and lightened. Through communing with Me, you transfer your heavy burdens to My strong shoulders. By gazing at Me, you gain My perspective on your life. This time alone with Me is essential for unscrambling your thoughts and smoothing out the day before you.

Be willing to fight for this precious time with Me. Opposition comes in many forms: your own desire to linger in bed; the evil one's determination to distract you from Me; the pressure of family, friends, and your own inner critic to spend your time more productively. As you grow in your desire to please Me above all else, you gain strength to resist these opponents. *Delight yourself in Me, for I am the deepest Desire of your heart.*

Within your temple, O God,
    we meditate on your unfailing love.

PSALM 48:9

Delight yourself in the LORD
    and he will give you the desires of your heart.

PSALM 37:4

FOR REFLECTION: DEUTERONOMY 33:12

SEEK MY FACE, and you will find all that you have longed for. The deepest yearnings of your heart are for intimacy with Me. I know, because I designed you to desire Me. Do not feel guilty about taking time to be still in My Presence. You are simply responding to the tugs of divinity within you. I made you in My image, and I hid heaven in your heart. Your yearning for Me is a form of homesickness: longing for your true home in heaven.

Do not be afraid to be different from other people. The path I have called you to travel is exquisitely right for you. The more closely you follow My leading, the more fully I can develop your gifts. To follow Me wholeheartedly, you must relinquish your desire to please other people. However, your closeness to Me will bless others by enabling you to shine brightly in this dark world.

As the deer pants for streams of water,
    so my soul pants for you, O God.
My soul thirsts for God, for the living God.
    When can I go and meet with God?

PSALM 42:1–2

Those who look to him are radiant;
    their faces are never covered with shame.

PSALM 34:5

FOR REFLECTION: PHILIPPIANS 2:15

TRUST ME by relinquishing control into My hands. *Let go, and recognize that I am God.* This is My world: I made it and I control it. Yours is a responsive part in the litany of Love. I search among My children for receptivity to Me. Guard well this gift that I have planted in your heart. Nurture it with the Light of My Presence.

When you bring Me prayer requests, lay out your concerns before Me. Speak to Me candidly; pour out your heart. Then thank Me for the answers that I have set into motion long before you can discern results. When your requests come to mind again, continue to thank Me for the answers that are on the way. If you keep on stating your concerns to Me, you will live in a state of tension. When you thank Me for how I am answering your prayers, your mind-set becomes much more positive. Thankful prayers keep your focus on My Presence and My promises.

Let be and be still, and know (recognize and understand) that I am God. I will be exalted among the nations! I will be exalted in the earth!

PSALM 46:10 (AMP)

His divine power has given us everything we need for life and godliness through our knowledge of him who called us by his own glory and goodness. Through these he has given us his very great and precious promises, so that through them you may participate in the divine nature and escape the corruption in the world caused by evil desires.

2 PETER 1:3–4

FOR REFLECTION: COLOSSIANS 4:2

I AM YOUR RISEN, LIVING SAVIOR! Through My resurrection *you have been born again to an ever-living hope.* It is vital for you to remain hopeful, no matter what is going on in your life. People put their hope in a variety of things—wealth, power, health, medical treatments—but these are all insufficient. When storms break upon your life, you can find only one adequate source of help—Me! The hope I provide is *an anchor for your soul, firm and secure* even in the most tempestuous waters. A good way to remain anchored in Me is to whisper as often as needed: "Jesus, You are my Hope." This affirmation strengthens you and keeps you connected to Me.

I am constantly working to transform your life. You need My help continually to keep your hope alive. I stand ready to help you at *all* times—during stormy episodes as well as times of smooth sailing. I am not only *ever-living* but also more abundantly alive than you can possibly imagine. There are no limits to what *My great Power and Glory* can accomplish! I can change the most "hopeless" situation into outright victory. Moreover, as you affirm your trust in Me—no matter how difficult your circumstances—I am able to transform you: gradually, lovingly. *Those who hope in Me will not be disappointed.*

———⇒✦⇐———

Then they will see the Son of Man coming in the clouds with great power and glory.

MARK 13:26 (NKJV)

FOR REFLECTION: 1 PETER 1:3 (AMP);
HEBREWS 6:19; ISAIAH 49:23B

I AM ABLE TO KEEP YOU FROM STUMBLING. I know how weak you are: how easily you would stumble if I were not holding on to you. I can also *present you faultless before the Presence of My Glory.* You are growing in grace, but complete freedom from sin will not be possible until you leave this fallen world. Nonetheless, because you truly trust Me as Savior I *keep you from stumbling* in the ultimate sense: I won't let you lose your salvation.

I am able to present you faultless—blameless, perfect, unblemished—before the Presence of My Glory because *I have clothed you with garments of salvation and arrayed you in a robe of righteousness.* I want you to wear this royal robe with confidence. You are absolutely secure because it is *My* righteousness that saves you—not yours.

Exceeding Joy is for both you and Me. I delight in you now, but this Joy will be astronomically magnified when you join Me in Glory. The Joy you will experience in heaven is so far beyond anything you have known on earth that it is indescribable. Nothing can rob you of this glorious inheritance which is *imperishable and will not fade away.* Rejoice!

Now to Him who is able to keep you from stumbling, and to present you faultless before the presence of His glory with exceeding joy, to God our Savior, who alone is wise, be glory and majesty, dominion and power, both now and forevermore. Amen.

JUDE 24–25 (NKJV)

FOR REFLECTION: ISAIAH 61:10; 1 PETER 1:3–4 (NASB)

I KNOW THE PLANS I HAVE FOR YOU, plans to prosper you and not to harm you, plans to give you hope and a future. This promise provides a feast of encouragement—offering you prosperity, hope, and a blessed future. Because the world is so fractured and full of pain, people tend to think dark thoughts and feel hopeless about the future. Unless you stay alert, you are vulnerable to such thoughts and feelings too. This makes you easy prey for *your adversary, the devil, who prowls about like a roaring lion, seeking someone to devour.* I gave My body on the cross to provide eternal nourishment for you, but the evil one wants to devour you! The contrast is crystal-clear, and the stakes are immeasurably high.

Mankind has a voracious appetite for finding out what the future will bring. Astrologers and fortune-tellers capitalize on this lust to peer into *secret things—things that belong to Me.* However, to feast on Me you must live in the present moment. This is where you can encounter Me and enjoy My Presence. As you come to the table of My delights, be sure to bring your fork of trust and your spoon of thankfulness. Take plenty of time enjoying Me, and your *soul will delight in the richest of fare.*

———————

"Why spend money on what is not bread, and your labor on what does not satisfy? Listen, listen to me, and eat what is good, and your soul will delight in the richest of fare."

ISAIAH 55:2

FOR REFLECTION: JEREMIAH 29:11;
1 PETER 5:8 (NASB); DEUTERONOMY 29:29 (NKJV)

HOPE IS A GOLDEN CORD connecting you to heaven. This cord helps you hold your head up high, even when multiple trials are buffeting you. I never leave your side, and I never let go of your hand. But without the cord of hope, your head may slump and your feet may shuffle as you journey uphill with Me. Hope lifts your perspective from your weary feet to the glorious view you can see from the high road. You are reminded that the road we're traveling together is ultimately a highway to heaven. When you consider this radiant destination, the roughness or smoothness of the road ahead becomes much less significant. I am training you to hold in your heart a dual focus: My continual Presence and the hope of heaven.

Be joyful in hope, patient in affliction, faithful in prayer.

ROMANS 12:12

But since we belong to the day, let us be self-controlled, putting on faith and love as a breastplate, and the hope of salvation as a helmet.

1 THESSALONIANS 5:8

God did this so that, by two unchangeable things in which it is impossible for God to lie, we who have fled to take hold of the hope offered to us may be greatly encouraged. We have this hope as an anchor for the soul, firm and secure. It enters the inner sanctuary behind the curtain.

HEBREWS 6:18–19

NOTHING CAN SEPARATE YOU from My Love. Let this divine assurance trickle through your mind and into your heart and soul. Whenever you start to feel fearful or anxious, repeat this unconditional promise: "Nothing can separate me from Your Love, Jesus."

Most of mankind's misery stems from feeling unloved. In the midst of adverse circumstances, people tend to feel that love has been withdrawn and they have been forsaken. This feeling of abandonment is often worse than the adversity itself. Be assured that I never abandon any of My children, not even temporarily. *I will never leave you or forsake you!* My Presence watches over you continually. *I have engraved you on the palms of My hands.*

———◦◦◦———

For I am convinced that neither death nor life, neither angels nor demons, neither the present nor the future, nor any powers, neither height nor depth, nor anything else in all creation, will be able to separate us from the love of God that is in Christ Jesus our Lord.

ROMANS 8:38–39

No one will be able to stand up against you all the days of your life. As I was with Moses, so I will be with you; I will never leave you nor forsake you.

JOSHUA 1:5

FOR REFLECTION: ISAIAH 49:15–16

WEAR MY ROBE OF RIGHTEOUSNESS with ease. I custom-made it for you, to cover you from head to toe. The price I paid for this covering was astronomical—My own blood. You could never purchase such a royal garment, no matter how hard you worked. Sometimes you forget that My righteousness is a gift, and you feel ill at ease in your regal robe. I weep when I see you squirming under the velvety fabric, as if it were made of scratchy sackcloth.

I want you to trust Me enough to realize your privileged position in My kingdom. Relax in the luxuriant folds of your magnificent robe. Keep your eyes on Me, as you practice walking in this garment of righteousness. When your behavior is unfitting for one in My kingdom, do not try to throw off your royal robe. Instead, throw off the unrighteous behavior. Then you will be able to feel at ease in this glorious garment, enjoying the gift I fashioned for you before the foundation of the world.

I delight greatly in the LORD; my soul rejoices in my God. For he has clothed me with garments of salvation and arrayed me in a robe of righteousness, as a bridegroom adorns his head like a priest, and as a bride adorns herself with her jewels.

ISAIAH 61:10

You were taught, with regard to your former way of life, to put off your old self, which is being corrupted by its deceitful desires; to be made new in the attitude of your minds; and to put on the new self, created to be like God in true righteousness and holiness.

EPHESIANS 4:22–24

FOR REFLECTION: 2 CORINTHIANS 5:21

THANKFULNESS OPENS THE DOOR to My Presence. Though I am always with you, I have gone to great measures to preserve your freedom of choice. I have placed a door between you and Me, and I have empowered you to open or close that door. There are many ways to open it, but a grateful attitude is one of the most effective.

Thankfulness is built on a substructure of trust. When thankful words stick in your throat, you need to check up on your foundation of trust. When thankfulness flows freely from your heart and lips, let your gratitude draw you closer to Me. I want you to learn the art of *giving thanks in all circumstances.* See how many times you can thank Me daily; this will awaken your awareness to a multitude of blessings. It will also cushion the impact of trials when they come against you. Practice My Presence by practicing the discipline of thankfulness.

Enter his gates with thanksgiving
and his courts with praise;
give thanks to him and praise his name.

PSALM 100:4

Give thanks in all circumstances, for this is God's will for you in Christ Jesus.

1 THESSALONIANS 5:18

OPEN YOUR MIND AND HEART—your entire being—to receive My Love in full measure. So many of My children limp through their lives starved for Love, because they haven't learned the art of receiving. This is essentially an act of faith: believing that I love you with boundless, everlasting Love. The art of receiving is also a discipline: training your mind to trust Me, coming close to Me with confidence.

Remember that the evil one is *the father of lies*. Learn to recognize his deceptive intrusions into your thoughts. One of his favorite deceptions is to undermine your confidence in My unconditional Love. Fight back against these lies! Do not let them go unchallenged. *Resist the devil in My Name, and he will slink away from you. Draw near to Me,* and My Presence will envelop you in Love.

———

Therefore, since we have a great high priest who has gone through the heavens, Jesus the Son of God, let us hold firmly to the faith we profess. For we do not have a high priest who is unable to sympathize with our weaknesses, but we have one who has been tempted in every way, just as we are—yet was without sin. Let us then approach the throne of grace with confidence, so that we may receive mercy and find grace to help us in our time of need.

HEBREWS 4:14–16

FOR REFLECTION: EPHESIANS 3:16–19;
JOHN 8:44; JAMES 4:7–8 (NKJV)

A THANKFUL ATTITUDE opens windows of heaven. Spiritual blessings fall freely onto you through those openings into eternity. Moreover, as you look up with a grateful heart, you get glimpses of Glory through those windows. You cannot yet live in heaven, but you can experience foretastes of your ultimate home. Such samples of heavenly fare revive your hope. Thankfulness opens you up to these experiences, which then provide further reasons to be grateful. Thus, your path becomes an upward spiral: ever increasing in gladness.

Thankfulness is not some sort of magic formula; it is the language of Love, which enables you to communicate intimately with Me. A thankful mind-set does not entail a denial of reality with its plethora of problems. Instead, it *rejoices in Me, your Savior,* in the midst of trials and tribulations. *I am your refuge and strength, an ever-present and well-proved help in trouble.*

—————

God is our Refuge and Strength [mighty and impenetrable to temptation], a very present and well-proved help in trouble.

PSALM 46:1 (AMP)

FOR REFLECTION: HABAKKUK 3:17–18

BE CONTENT TO BE ONE OF MY SHEEP—eternally known, eternally secure. I want you to *hear My voice*, so you can *follow Me* closely all the days and moments of your life. I speak to you in many ways, though most clearly through My Word. You need to maintain a listening attitude in order to hear Me. This requires both patience and perseverance: waiting in My Presence, eager to hear from Me. I, your Shepherd-King, not only lead you through each day of your life; I also open to you the gates of heaven. You do well to remember that the Shepherd who so tenderly leads you is the King of eternity.

Though your earth-body will someday die, you yourself *will never perish*. When you become *absent from the body*, you will *be present with Me* in a deep, rich, glorious way beyond anything you can imagine! No one will be able to *snatch you out of My hand*. This assurance of your eternal destiny sets you free from fear of death. It also strengthens you to live bountifully today—joyously following your Shepherd.

Sheep are not designed to live independently. They need a wise, loving shepherd to guide them carefully. Similarly, you live best when you follow Me humbly, in sheep-like fashion. As you trust Me to know what is best for you, I lovingly *guide you in paths of righteousness*.

"My sheep hear My voice, and I know them, and they follow Me. And I give them eternal life, and they shall never perish; neither shall anyone snatch them out of My hand."

JOHN 10:27–28 (NKJV)

FOR REFLECTION: 2 CORINTHIANS 5:8 (NKJV); PSALM 23:1–3

I AM THE GIFT that continuously gives—bounteously, with no strings attached. Unconditional Love is such a radical concept that even My most devoted followers fail to grasp it fully. Absolutely nothing in heaven or on earth can cause Me to stop loving you. You may *feel* more loved when you are performing according to your expectations. But My Love for you is perfect; therefore it is not subject to variation. What *does* vary is your awareness of My loving Presence.

When you are dissatisfied with your behavior, you tend to feel unworthy of My Love. You may unconsciously punish yourself by withdrawing from Me and attributing the distance between us to My displeasure. Instead of returning to Me and receiving My Love, you attempt to earn My approval by trying harder. All the while, I am aching to hold you in *My everlasting arms,* to enfold you in My Love. When you are feeling unworthy or unloved, come to Me. Then ask for receptivity to *My unfailing Love.*

God is love. Whoever lives in love lives in God, and God in him. In this way, love is made complete among us so that we will have confidence on the day of judgment, because in this world we are like him. There is no fear in love. But perfect love drives out fear, because fear has to do with punishment. The one who fears is not made perfect in love.

1 JOHN 4:16–18

FOR REFLECTION: DEUTERONOMY 33:27; PSALM 13:5

I AM PERPETUALLY WITH YOU, taking care of you. That is the most important fact of your existence. I am not limited by time or space; My Presence with you is a forever-promise. You need not fear the future, for I am already there. When you make that *quantum leap* into eternity, you will find Me awaiting you in heaven. Your future is in My hands; I release it to you day by day, moment by moment. Therefore, *do not worry about tomorrow.*

I want you to live this day abundantly, seeing all there is to see, doing all there is to do. Don't be distracted by future concerns. Leave them to Me! Each day of life is a glorious gift, but so few people know how to live within the confines of today. Much of their energy for abundant living spills over the time line into tomorrow's worries or past regrets. Their remaining energy is sufficient only for limping through the day, not for living it to the full. I am training you to keep your focus on My Presence in the present. This is how to receive abundant Life, which flows freely from My throne of grace.

Therefore do not worry about tomorrow, for tomorrow will worry about itself. Each day has enough trouble of its own.

MATTHEW 6:34

Now listen, you who say, "Today or tomorrow we will go to this or that city, spend a year there, carry on business and make money." Why, you do not even know what will happen tomorrow. What is your life? You are a mist that appears for a little while and then vanishes. Instead, you ought to say, "If it is the Lord's will, we will live and do this or that."

JAMES 4:13–15

FOR REFLECTION: JOHN 10:10

I AM ALL AROUND YOU, hovering over you even as you seek My Face. I am nearer than you dare believe, closer than the air you breathe. If My children could only recognize My Presence, they would never feel lonely again. *I know every thought before you think it, every word before you speak it.* My Presence impinges on your innermost being. Can you see the absurdity of trying to hide anything from Me? You can easily deceive other people, and even yourself; but I read you like an open, large-print book.

Deep within themselves, most people have some awareness of My imminent Presence. Many people run from Me and vehemently deny My existence, because My closeness terrifies them. But My own children have nothing to fear, for I have cleansed them by My blood and clothed them in My righteousness. Be blessed by My intimate nearness. Since I live in you, let Me also live through you, shining My Light into the darkness.

———————

O LORD, you have searched me
    and you know me.
You know when I sit and when I rise;
    you perceive my thoughts from afar.
You discern my going out and my lying down;
    you are familiar with all my ways.
Before a word is on my tongue
    you know it completely, O LORD.

PSALM 139:1–4

FOR REFLECTION: EPHESIANS 2:13; 2 CORINTHIANS 5:21

I AM WITH YOU IN ALL THAT YOU DO, even in the most menial task. I am always aware of you, concerned with every detail of your life. Nothing escapes My notice—not even *the number of hairs on your head*. However, your awareness of My Presence falters and flickers; as a result, your life experience feels fragmented. When your focus is broad enough to include Me in your thoughts, you feel safe and complete. When your perception narrows so that problems or details fill your consciousness, you feel empty and incomplete.

Learn to look steadily at Me in all your moments and all your circumstances. Though the world is unstable and in flux, you can experience continuity through your uninterrupted awareness of My Presence. *Fix your gaze on what is unseen*, even as the visible world parades before your eyes.

———❦———

"Are not two sparrows sold for a penny? Yet not one of them will fall to the ground apart from the will of your Father. And even the very hairs of your head are all numbered. So don't be afraid; you are worth more than many sparrows."

MATTHEW 10:29–31

So we fix our eyes not on what is seen, but on what is unseen. For what is seen is temporary, but what is unseen is eternal.

2 CORINTHIANS 4:18

FOR REFLECTION: HEBREWS 11:27

FORGET THE FORMER THINGS; DO NOT DWELL ON THE PAST. See, I am doing a new thing! I am a God of surprises—infinitely more creative than you can imagine. The universe displays some of My creativity, but there is more—much more. I am making *a new heaven and a new earth.* Moreover, I am preparing My people—all around the world—to live there with Me in endless ecstasy. Let this eternal perspective strengthen and encourage you.

As you journey along your life-path with Me, refuse to let the past define you or your expectations of what lies ahead. You may feel as if the road you are on is tiresome or even a dead end. That is because you're projecting the past into the future. The road-block you are straining to see up ahead is really just an illusion. The future is in My hands, and I can do surprising things with it!

Your gravest danger is giving up: ceasing to believe I can still do wondrous new things in you and your world. Your assignment is to keep moving forward in trusting dependence on Me. Stop focusing on obstacles you might encounter, and concentrate on staying in touch with Me. As you continue taking steps of trust, expect the path before you to open up in refreshing newness. *I am making a way in the desert and streams in the wasteland.*

Then I saw a new heaven and a new earth, for the first heaven and the first earth had passed away, and there was no longer any sea.

REVELATION 21:1

FOR REFLECTION: ISAIAH 43:18–19;
EPHESIANS 3:20; PSALM 25:4 (NKJV)

I GIVE YOU HOPE—hope that the best part of your life is not behind you. Rather, it stretches out before you gloriously: into an eternity of experiences that will get better and better and better. For now, though, you inhabit a world of *death, sorrow, crying, and pain.* Let the hope of heaven empower you to live well in this broken world that is passing away. In heaven *I will wipe away every tear from your eyes*—permanently!

If this world were all there is, it would be tragic beyond description. When *the day of the Lord* comes, I will destroy the entire universe as you know it. And I will replace it with a new universe where My followers will live forever in ceaseless ecstasy. Let this hope give you courage to keep holding your head up high as you endure suffering and sorrow.

The best part of your life lies ahead—stored up for you in heaven, awaiting your arrival. This is true for all Christians, both young and old. As you grow older and deal with infirmities, you may feel as if your life is closing in on you. Physically, your limitations do increase with age and illness. However, your spiritual life can open up ever wider as your soul grows strong in the nourishing Light of My Presence. When you "graduate" to heaven, your soul-Joy will instantly expand—exponentially! *Blessed is the one who will eat at the feast in the kingdom of God.*

And God will wipe away every tear from their eyes; there shall be no more death, nor sorrow, nor crying. There shall be no more pain, for the former things have passed away.

REVELATION 21:4 (NKJV)

FOR REFLECTION: JOEL 1:15; LUKE 14:15

I AM YOURS FOR ALL ETERNITY. *I am the Alpha and the Omega: the One who is and was and is to come.* The world you inhabit is a place of constant changes—more than your mind can absorb without going into shock. Even the body you inhabit is changing relentlessly, in spite of modern science's attempts to prolong youth and life indefinitely. *I, however, am the same yesterday and today and forever.*

Because I never change, your relationship with Me provides a rock-solid foundation for your life. I will never leave your side. When you move on from this life to the next, My Presence beside you will shine brighter with each step. You have nothing to fear, because I am with you for all time and throughout eternity.

"I am the Alpha and the Omega," says the Lord God, "who is, and who was, and who is to come, the Almighty."

REVELATION 1:8

Jesus Christ is the same yesterday and today and forever.

HEBREWS 13:8

For this God is our God for ever and ever;
    he will be our guide even to the end.

PSALM 48:14

FOR REFLECTION: PSALM 102:25–27

I AM THE *PRINCE OF PEACE*. As I said to My disciples, I say also to you: *Peace be with you.* Since I am your constant Companion, My Peace is steadfastly with you. When you keep your focus on Me, you experience both My Presence and My Peace. Worship Me as King of kings, Lord of lords, and Prince of Peace.

You need My Peace each moment to accomplish My purposes in your life. Sometimes you are tempted to take shortcuts, in order to reach your goal as quickly as possible. But if the short-cut requires turning your back on My peaceful Presence, you must choose the longer route. Walk with Me along paths of Peace; enjoy the journey in My Presence.

———————

On the evening of that first day of the week, when the disciples were together, with the doors locked for fear of the Jews, Jesus came and stood among them and said, "Peace be with you!" After he said this, he showed them his hands and side. The disciples were overjoyed when they saw the Lord. Again Jesus said, "Peace be with you! As the Father has sent me, I am sending you."

JOHN 20:19–21

Show me Your ways, O LORD;
     teach me Your paths.

PSALM 25:4 (NKJV)

FOR REFLECTION: ISAIAH 9:6

I AM KING OF KINGS and Lord of lords, dwelling in dazzlingly bright Light! I am also your Shepherd, Companion, and Friend—the One who never lets go of your hand. Worship Me in My holy Majesty; come close to Me, and rest in My Presence. You need Me both as God and as Man. Only My Incarnation on that first, long-ago Christmas could fulfill your neediness. Since I went to such extreme measures to save you from your sins, you can be assured that I will *graciously give you all you need.*

Nurture well your trust in Me as Savior, Lord, and Friend. I have held back nothing in My provision for you. I have even deigned to live within you! Rejoice in all that I have done for you, and My Light will shine through you into the world.

Which God will bring about in his own time—God, the blessed and only Ruler, the King of kings and Lord of lords, who alone is immortal and who lives in unapproachable light, whom no one has seen or can see. To him be honor and might forever. Amen.

1 TIMOTHY 6:15–16

He who did not spare his own Son, but gave him up for us all—how will he not also, along with him, graciously give us all things?

ROMANS 8:32

And we have the word of the prophets made more certain, and you will do well to pay attention to it, as to a light shining in a dark place, until the day dawns and the morning star rises in your hearts.

2 PETER 1:19

FOR REFLECTION: PSALM 95:6–7

I AM WITH YOU ALWAYS. These were the last words I spoke before ascending into heaven. I continue to proclaim this promise to all who will listen. People respond to My continual Presence in various ways. Most Christians accept this teaching as truth but ignore it in their daily living. Some ill-taught or wounded believers fear (and may even resent) My awareness of all they do, say, and think. A few people center their lives around this glorious promise and find themselves blessed beyond all expectations.

When My Presence is the focal point of your consciousness, all the pieces of your life fall into place. As you gaze at Me through the eyes of your heart, you can see the world around you from My perspective. The fact that *I am with you* makes every moment of your life meaningful.

————

"And teaching them to obey everything I have commanded you. And surely I am with you always, to the very end of the age."

MATTHEW 28:20

O LORD, you have searched me
    and you know me.
You know when I sit and when I rise;
    you perceive my thoughts from afar.
You discern my going out and my lying down;
    you are familiar with all my ways.
Before a word is on my tongue
    you know it completely, O LORD.

PSALM 139:1–4

If you liked reading this booklet, you may enjoy
these other titles by *Sarah Young*

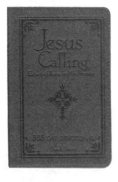

ISBN 978-1-4041-8782-5

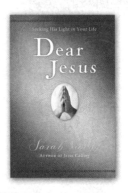

ISBN: 978-1-4041-0495-2

ISBN 978-1-4041-8695-8

ISBN: 978-1-4003-1634-2

Thomas Nelson
Since 1798